METRO-GOLDWYN-MAYER
PRESENTS

Mutiny on the Bounty

AN ARCOLA PICTURE

4

Catching fish with stones and palm leaves

"Because of these magic islands we may never be the same."

COUNTLESS HUNDREDS, among them explorer Captain Cook, writer Robert Louis Stevenson and artist Paul Gauguin, have been inspired to use those words following visits to the Polynesian Islands.

The thousands upon thousands of islands, some small, some large, that dot the South Pacific Ocean have provided the setting for many of history's most dramatic events—and some of its most romantic legends as well.

A few, like those that comprise the Hawaiian and the Philippine groups, have been attracting tourists for years. Others, like Saipan, Iwo Jima and Kwajelein, became household words during World War II. Still others like Fiji, Pago Pago and Moorea, have gained renown through writers like Maugham and Michener.

Now two of the most famous of them all—the islands of Tahiti and Pitcairn—are destined to become even more celebrated through MUTINY ON THE BOUNTY. These two tiny islands figure prominently

in the story of Captain Bligh and Fletcher Christian; both islands, in fact, owe at least a share of their fame to the mutiny itself. Except for their remoteness, their beauty and their connection with the historic event, the two share little in common.

Tahiti, for generations, has been the dream island of the Western World, a land of easygoing funloving people, a land that has represented escape from civilization. On the other hand, Pitcairn, perched high on a rock that juts 700 feet out of the ocean, is home to a people famed as God fearing, hard working and sober minded men and women.

For almost a year, members of the MUTINY ON THE BOUNTY company lived among the Tahitians and like the Cooks, the Stevensons, the Gauguins, and the real Bounty mutineers who preceded them, they admitted they may never be quite the same again.

What is it about this legendary island that has set it apart from other places in the world, some of which must surely approach it in beauty? What, as a matter

(continued on page 8)

A Moment from History

THE TRUE STORY upon which MUTINY ON THE BOUNTY is based actually began on December 23, 1787.

It was then H.M.S. Bounty sailed from Spithead, England, under orders to proceed to Otaheite (later changed to Tahiti) in the South Seas, there to take on breadfruit for transport to the West Indies.

Early explorers, including Captain Cook, had brought back fabulous tales of this strange looking plant that appeared to be the principal staple of diet for the strong, vigorous people who lived on the South Pacific islands.

Colonists in the British West Indies reasoned that this extraordinary plant might provide a cheap and nourishing food for their African slaves. They petitioned King George III to have the tree introduced into the colonies and the Bounty, under command of William Bligh, was commissioned to find and

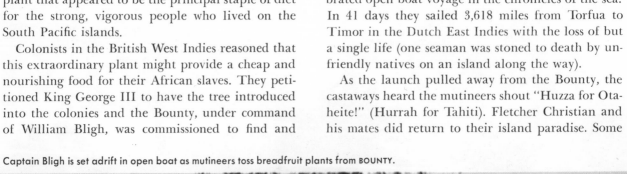

transplant the unusual tree.

The Bounty and her crew stayed in Tahiti more than four months. After the breadfruit plants had been safely stored aboard, she began the long voyage to Jamaica.

While passing through Endeavor Strait, off the island of Torfua, the vessel became the scene of history's most famous mutiny. Taking command of the ship, Fletcher Christian set Captain Bligh adrift in a boat only 23 feet long.

The incredible Bligh and eighteen of his supporters then performed the most celebrated open boat voyage in the chronicles of the sea. In 41 days they sailed 3,618 miles from Torfua to Timor in the Dutch East Indies with the loss of but a single life (one seaman was stoned to death by unfriendly natives on an island along the way).

As the launch pulled away from the Bounty, the castaways heard the mutineers shout "Huzza for Otaheite!" (Hurrah for Tahiti). Fletcher Christian and his mates did return to their island paradise. Some

Captain Bligh is set adrift in open boat as mutineers toss breadfruit plants from BOUNTY.

"Mr. Bligh, I'm taking command of this ship . . ."

elected to remain there, while the rest threw in their lot with Christian and a handful of natives.

This small group sailed from Tahiti on a moonlight night and the world was not to learn of its fate until eighteen years later when the *Topaz*, out of Boston, touched at Pitcairn Island, a lonely rock 1,300 miles southeast of Tahiti.

Mathew Fogler, skipper of the ship, discovered Christian had taken his men to Pitcairn, where they had run the Bounty aground and burned her.

Within months, trouble over the division of land and women had touched off a wave of violence, and when the *Topaz* arrived in 1808 only one of the mutineers remained alive. He was permitted to remain there and live out his life with the surviving women and the children of the mutineers, descendants of whom still live on the island today.

Safely back in England, meanwhile, Captain Bligh faced a court martial and was absolved of blame for loss of his ship. He was, however, censured by the court for the harsh treatment of his men. The British dispatched another vessel, the *Pandora*, to Tahiti, where the mutineers who had remained there (except for two who had died during the year and a half on the island) were taken aboard and placed in irons.

Four of these lost their lives when the *Pandora* was wrecked in a violent storm on the return voyage. Of those who finally returned to England ten were brought to trial. Four were acquitted; three were court martialed but subsequently pardoned. And three (John Millward, Thomas Burkitt and Thomas Ellison) paid the supreme penalty and were hanged as enemies of the Crown.

This is the true story upon which the film is based.

Breadfruit ready for transplanting

"I hope I shall be amused, sir . . . but it does seem a difficult dance . . ."

(continued from page 5)

of fact is the island of Tahiti?

With its sister isles, Moorea (12 miles away) and Bora Bora (150 miles distant), on both of which the MUTINY ON THE BOUNTY company worked, Tahiti is a part of the Society Island group. There are five such groups that comprise the hundred or more islands stretching across the heart of the South Pacific and known as French Polynesia.

It is not definitely established who were the first Europeans to discover Tahiti. However, it is known that as early as 1605, Spanish explorers sailed among the Society Islands, and it is believed some of them may have touched at Tahiti.

In 1767, the first formal possession of the island was made by the English navigator, Captain Wallis,

in the name of King George III. Some months later, the French navigator, de Bougainville, unaware of Wallis' action, claimed Tahiti as a French possession. In 1769 Captain Cook arrived with a group of scientists on *H.M.S. Endeaver* to observe the transit of the planet Venus across the sun.

Next to come were Spaniards from Peru in 1772. They founded a small settlement, but abandoned it three years later. In 1788 Captain Bligh arrived on *H.M.S. Bounty*.

In the years that followed, many ships from European countries visited Tahiti's shores. Among them was a shipload of English missionaries who established the first mission on the island in 1797. The French Catholics sought to establish a mission of

"This island is inhabited by over two hundred thousand savages . . ."

their own in 1836 but were refused permission by Queen Pomare IV.

The resulting conflict finally was resolved when Admiral du Petit Thouars took possession of Tahiti in the name of France in 1842. In 1880 King Pomare V relinquished all control of island affairs to the French government and since that time the island has been under the administration of France.

Tahiti covers an area about one tenth the size of Greater Los Angeles. The total population is about 40,000 of whom half live in the only town—Papeete.

The interior of the island is unpopulated—an almost trackless wilderness of peaks and valleys, crags, gorges and plunging waterfalls.

A circuit of the island, along 90 miles of twisting

The new BOUNTY in exact spot where Bligh anchored original vessel

Paul Gauguin

Captain Cook

Robert Louis Stevenson

coastal road, has been described as a true journey through a tropical Land of Oz. Palm trees are everywhere and, among them, mango and breadfruit, avocado and banana in prodigal profusion. But, as breathtaking as is the loveliness to be found on every side in Tahiti, it is the people themselves who set the island undeniably apart. Travel folders describe them simply as "Happy, friendly and carefree — living where there is no time, no tomorrow, only today."

Indeed, there is little need for the Tahitian to devote too many hours to the drudgery of working for a living. Fruits of every description hang on thousands of trees, ready for picking. Clothing is used for decorum—because it never gets colder than 65 degrees and rarely warmer than 86 degrees.

Thirteen hundred miles to the south of Tahiti, halfway between New Zealand and Panama, lies Pitcairn. On this tiny island (it is two miles long and one mile wide) live 153 people who manage very nicely without telephones, automobiles or the airplane. There are no taxes, no customs duties and no monthly bills to meet.

There is no unemployment because all work is divided evenly. There is a jail but citizens are sent in only to sweep it out. No one on the island can recall a major crime and the words juvenile and delinquency are yet to be linked.

Flowers, fruits and fish of every kind are there for taking. The climate is temperate with sea breezes keeping the temperature pleasant most of the time. The Bounty mutineers believed—and they were right —that there could be no escape from Pitcairn, which was uninhabited when they settled there. The descendants of the mutineers live on Pitcairn today.

Because there is no natural harbor, ships must anchor far off the island's shore and only do so occasionally. When a ship stops, the islanders row out in small boats to get the mail, to sell trinkets and fruit to the passengers and to exchange news.

Pitcairn belongs to England (the people speak a curious 18th Century English) but the British leave the islanders to rule themselves, a job they have managed very well over the years, or ever since 1856 when the government, thinking Pitcairn too crowded and not suitable for colonization, moved everyone to Norfolk Island. But within ten years most of the Pitcairners had moved back and they have stayed there ever since.

The people on Pitcairn are deeply religious. When John Tay, an American missionary, arrived in 1886 he converted everyone to Seventh Day Adventism and since that time there has never been any other religious influence on the island. The word of the church is law. When the community bell sounds three times, all able bodied men, from 16 to 60, must report to the courthouse and do whatever work the island council decides must be done—road mending, land clearing, etc.

When the people on Pitcairn learned that a film based on the adventures of their ancestors was being produced, they sent a cable to MGM offering their cooperation. They are very proud of the part Fletcher Christian and his mates played in helping achieve better officer-seamen relations in the British Navy.

Pitcairn and Tahiti are both famous because of an historic event. Yet two islands whose people and customs are farther apart could hardly be imagined. The strong willed Pitcairners long ago outlawed alcohol and all stimulating drinks from their island. Even coffee and tea are taboo. Their most sacred possession is a Holy Bible saved from the Bounty.

Tahiti is a land that inspired writer Barnaby Conrad to report: "I've come to the conclusion that the only truly wacky people in the world are those who, given a choice, are foolish enough ever to leave this benighted, this wonderful, this unique, this beautiful and—all right—this wonderfully wacky island."

"Happy, friendly, carefree."

A Global Project

THE making of MUTINY ON THE BOUNTY became, by the time the film was completed, a truly global project.

Its cast came from England, Ireland, Scotland, Australia, California and the islands of Tahiti and Bora Bora. Its crew of technicians was flown to the location sites from Paris, London and Hollywood.

The ship which plays a central role in the story was built in Nova Scotia, with materials that went into her from all over the world. Her crew was mostly Canadian. Filming took place in some of the most remote areas of the South Pacific.

As soon as the decision was made to produce the film, the research department at MGM Studios began gathering the voluminous data needed to put the dramatic story on film.

At the library of the British Admiralty in London, other researchers began poring over records of the court martial and trial that followed the historic mutiny. They made copies of the original Bounty blueprints still preserved in England. These were later used by builders of the "new" Bounty.

The plan was to film most of the picture in and around Tahiti where the actual story had taken place. This required movement of large equipment and 125 men and women to the South Pacific; and the maintenance of this small army for many months.

Months before the cameras began turning, Aaron Rosenberg, who produced the film as an Arcola Production, went to London to visit the British Admiralty Library, the National Maritime Museum, and to confer with experts. He inspected the yellow pages of the actual log kept by Captain Bligh, the journals of Boatswain's Mate James Morrison and Master's Mate John Fryer. He had photographs made of clothing and equipment used by seamen of that day.

Six months before filming, the producer made a survey trip to Tahiti to select location sites. More than 200 preliminary set sketches were made for the production. Four large war canoes, each holding 40 oarsmen, were built. More than 1,000 additional native canoes had to be assembled.

For months during and after filming, magazines and newspapers had devoted many pages to the theme that with arrival of the jet (as many as eight a week began landing at the lone airport after the film was completed) Tahiti never would be the same.

The film unit left more than two million dollars with the islanders. Some 7,000 of them were employed in the film's production and all islanders had, in one way or another, been concerned with it. The man who once wrote that, "in Tahiti work is not illegal but the Tahitian regards it as a most peculiar way to

"We shall take all due military precautions . . ."

spend one's time," would have had to change his opinion had he been on the scene.

So anxious, indeed, were the natives to perform that on one occasion, when 5,000 were called for a scene depicting arrival of the Bounty at Matavaii Bay a total of 6,055 Tahitians showed up. "Take all or none!" was the edict of the chiefs who had assembled them from the various districts. All were taken, of course, and it was a source of satisfaction to the director and the cast to find that Tahitians took their acting assignments in a businesslike manner. They did

not wander from the set, as predicted, nor did they lose interest in what was in front of the camera.

The Tahitian seems to have the perfect way of life. His basic philosophy, that life must be lived as if there is no tomorrow, and that living means "to sing, to dance, to love" has not changed over the years. The men who mutinied against Captain Bligh found these things to be the charm of Tahiti. It is doubtful if the arrival of motion picture units or thousands of jet-borne tourists is likely to change the ways and the thinking of a unique people.

The Ship

🦢 **ONE OF THE MOST FAMOUS SHIPS** ever to sail the seas is H.M.S. Bounty, the three masted sailing vessel built expressly for the film. She attracted the attention and fame of a true motion picture star almost from the moment she began life, with the laying of her keel in Lunenburg, Nova Scotia, on a snowy February day in 1960.

So many tourists came to visit her during the seven months she was under construction that the Smith and Rhuland Shipyard, where she was built, had to hire a special guide to handle the crowds. On the day of her launching more than 20,000 persons descended on the little town to join in the festivities.

When she sailed for Tahiti more thousands lined

the harbor to wish her Godspeed. On the long voyage to the South Seas she was saluted by passing liners, including the Queen Mary. When she dropped anchor in Matavaii Bay, brown skinned girls bearing leis for her crew descended on her. Guitar strumming musicians boarded her and the Governor of all Polynesia was present to make her welcome.

Designed from actual plans of the original H.M.S. Bounty (from the British Admiralty Museum), she is the first ship ever built from the keel up especially for a motion picture. The usual practice has been to revamp the lines of a serviceable vessel to suit the needs of the script.

The blood of many generations of sea dogs runs warmly in the 2,908 residents of Lunenburg. Perhaps that is the reason they took more than ordinary pride that their largest shipyard was selected to build the new Bounty. In one way or another, practically everyone in the town had a hand in her construction.

Throughout the months of building, with crews working double shifts, they seemed to sense the same thrill of accomplishment that must have surged through the hearts of their forefathers when they sent onto the seas the sturdiest sailing vessels of the day.

Little Lunenburg, the home of hundreds of ships of the past, is one of the few places in the world today able to produce the rare skills needed to build this vessel. Indeed, so rare have become the skills needed for such a job that it is probable she will be the last wooden ship of her kind to be constructed anywhere in the world.

Above decks, the Bounty is a faithful copy of the original, from rope davits to 10,000 square feet of canvas on the square rigged masts. Captain Bligh's vessel was 85 feet long and carried a crew of 62. The new Bounty is 118 feet in length (an increase made necessary because of space required for movement of cameras during filming). Her beam is 30 feet, six inches, with a 14 foot draft. Her tonnage is 480 gross and 128 net.

More than 400,000 board feet of lumber, about half of it American oak from New Jersey, was used in her planking. The biggest timber used was in the main mast, which is 27 inches in diameter and 65 feet long.

Above the three masts that tower into the sky are the topmasts and staysails that help make her a thrilling sight. Her total height from the deck to top of the mainmast is 103 feet.

Two old-timers, Alfred Dauphinee and Charlie Hebb, were given two of the most important jobs of all. Dauphinee, a blockmaker and the only one left in Nova Scotia, was kept busy with his largest order

H.M.S. BOUNTY nears completion in Nova Scotia

Ready to sail from Lunenburg on great adventure

"You'll give no one water without my permission. Take that ladle below . . ."

of all time. He had to produce 250 blocks and more than 150 deadeyes for the ship's rigging. A block is a pulley and a deadeye is a round block of wood pierced with three holes and used for bracing the mast.

Seventy-year-old Hebb, who has spent his life as a sailmaker, had to make one concession to progress to take on the job of providing the 10,000 feet of canvas sail (largest task he had ever tackled). He had to buy an electric sewing machine. "I had to," says Charlie regretfully, "the whole job would have taken more than a year if I'd done it completely by hand."

Into the ship went, among other nautical items: 12 tons of screw bolts, 14 tons of bar iron, 2½ tons of spikes, 1,200 pounds of putty, 1½ miles of wire rigging, 10 miles of rope of various sizes, and 192 double and single rigging blocks.

Design and construction of the ship, which cost more than $700,000 to build, were under supervision of James Havens, veteran Hollywood director of motion picture sea sequences and himself a nautical architect.

Captain Ellsworth Coggins, retired commander of the Royal Canadian Navy, was selected to command the ship and placed in charge of the crew of 25, ranging in age from 19 to 72, who were chosen from hundreds of applicants.

The Bounty made the 7,327 mile voyage from Lunenburg to Tahiti, via the Panama Canal in 33 sailing days. She touched land only at Cristobal. Her average speed was 9.3 knots and she covered 269 miles on her fastest day's run. It took Captain Bligh more than a year to make the journey from England to Tahiti in 1787.

After filming was completed in Tahiti, the Bounty,

"Fletcher Christian is my name . . ."

"Like riding a cork over a waterfall it were, sir . . ."

under command of Captain Coggins, set sail for North America. When word arrived in Los Angeles that the famous vessel was but a few miles at sea, crowds of well-wishers began driving to the port of San Pedro to welcome her.

On the morning she passed into the inner harbor, thousands of spectators lined the wharves. Never in the history of the port, not even in the days of World War II when naval vessels would pay brief visits between sea battles, was a ship the object of such a greeting. The welcome lasted for days, with tourists from all parts of the nation visiting the ship.

Later, the Bounty began a world cruise, sailing northward with Vancouver and Victoria in British Columbia as the first ports of call. Once again, the welcoming crowds were huge. From the two Canadian cities the Bounty proceeded to pay an official visit to Seattle and the World's Fair. By the time the ship stopped at its fourth West Coast port, San Francisco, more than a million visitors had hailed her.

From the California coast, the Bounty once again sailed through the Panama Canal for visits to New Orleans and Miami. Then she moved up the Atlantic Seaboard and finally set sail across the Atlantic with

"Those mutineers must hang, you see. They must hang . . ."

"I dislike failure. I dislike it even more than the Admiralty does."

"A dozen with the lash will teach him better still . . ."

London and other foreign ports on her schedule.

Finally, her destination was New York, and her arrival was timed to coincide with the world premiere of MUTINY ON THE BOUNTY.

Everywhere along her course, the Bounty was greeted by thousands of people who agreed that this vessel deserves a place among the historic ships of the world. She lived in a modern day in the tradition of the first H.M.S. Bounty and sparked men's imaginations into recalling the most famous mutiny the world has ever known. ⚓ ⚓ ⚓

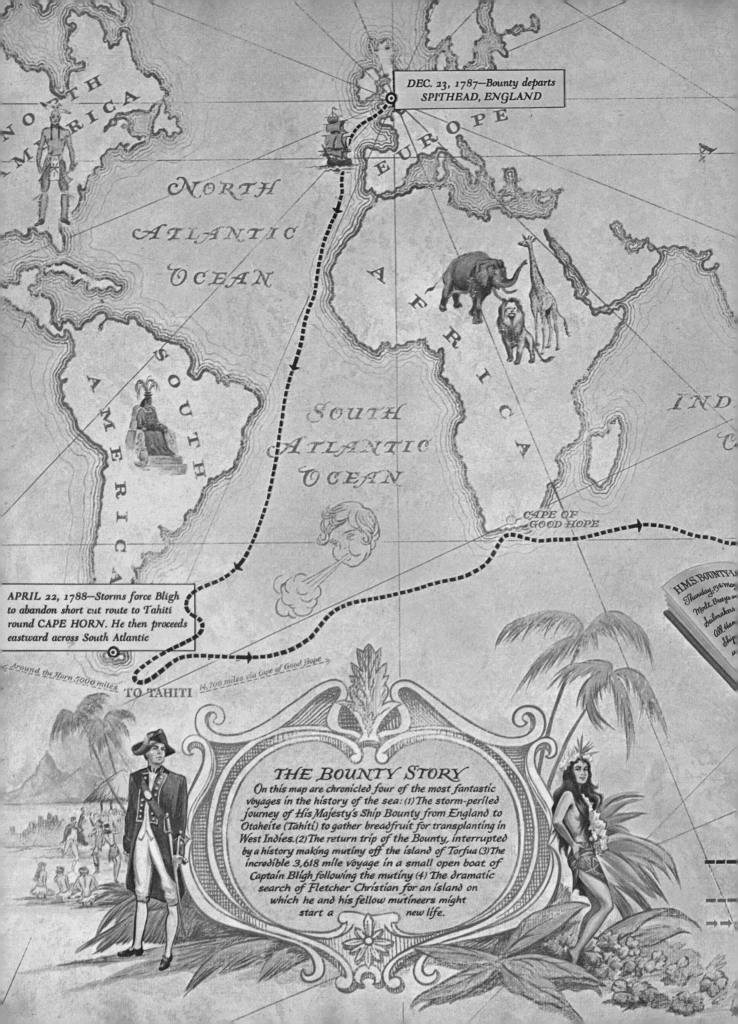

DEC. 23, 1787—Bounty departs
SPITHEAD, ENGLAND

NORTH AMERICA

NORTH ATLANTIC OCEAN

EUROPE

AFRICA

SOUTH AMERICA

SOUTH ATLANTIC OCEAN

IND...

CAPE OF GOOD HOPE

APRIL 22, 1788—Storms force Bligh
to abandon short cut route to Tahiti
round CAPE HORN. He then proceeds
eastward across South Atlantic

Around the Horn, 7000 miles

TO TAHITI   14,700 miles via Cape of Good Hope

H.M.S. BOUNTY L...
Thursday 15th ma...
Mod. Breeze a...
Sailmakers...
All Han...
Ship...

THE BOUNTY STORY
On this map are chronicled four of the most fantastic
voyages in the history of the sea: (1) The storm-periled
journey of His Majesty's Ship Bounty from England to
Otaheite (Tahiti) to gather breadfruit for transplanting in
West Indies. (2) The return trip of the Bounty, interrupted
by a history making mutiny off the island of Torfua (3) The
incredible 3,618 mile voyage in a small open boat of
Captain Bligh following the mutiny (4) The dramatic
search of Fletcher Christian for an island on
which he and his fellow mutineers might
start a   new life.

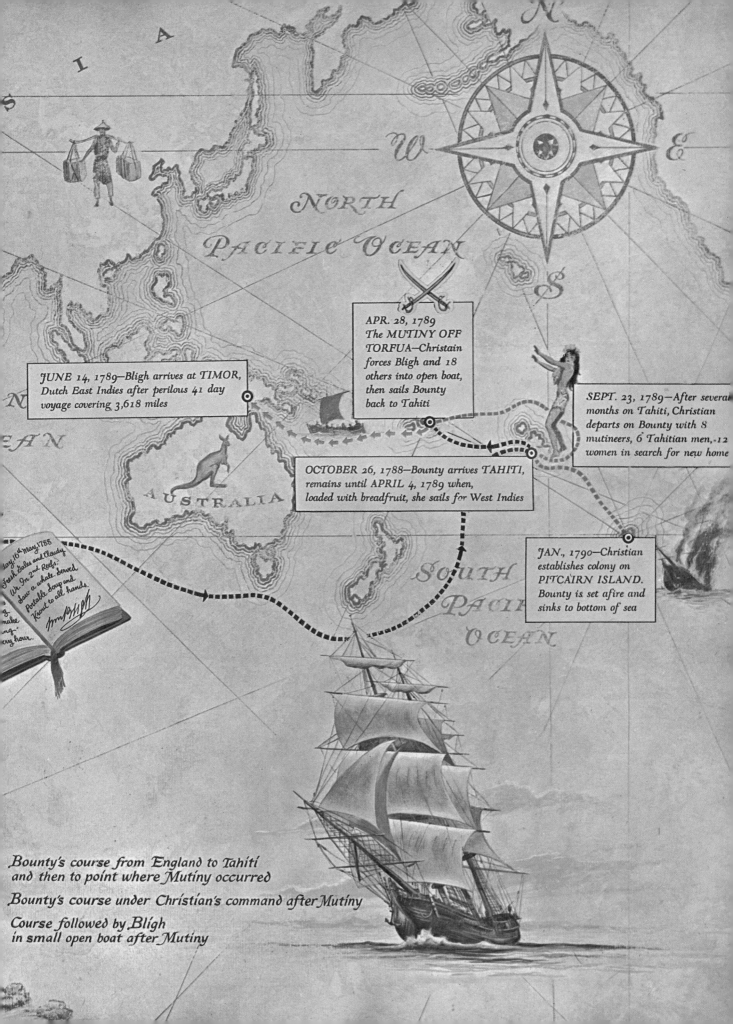

ASIA

NORTH

PACIFIC OCEAN

JUNE 14, 1789—Bligh arrives at TIMOR, Dutch East Indies after perilous 41 day voyage covering 3,618 miles

APR. 28, 1789
The MUTINY OFF TORFUA—Christain forces Bligh and 18 others into open boat, then sails Bounty back to Tahiti

SEPT. 23, 1789—After several months on Tahiti, Christian departs on Bounty with 8 mutineers, 6 Tahitian men, 12 women in search for new home

OCTOBER 26, 1788—Bounty arrives TAHITI, remains until APRIL 4, 1789 when, loaded with breadfruit, she sails for West Indies

AUSTRALIA

JAN., 1790—Christian establishes colony on PITCAIRN ISLAND. Bounty is set afire and sinks to bottom of sea

SOUTH
PACIFIC
OCEAN

Bounty's course from England to Tahiti and then to point where Mutiny occurred

Bounty's course under Christian's command after Mutiny

Course followed by Bligh in small open boat after Mutiny

MARLON BRANDO: Fletcher Christian

One famous critic recently wrote: "he can chew on a matchstick with more skill than many actors can summon up to create a whole character, and simply watching him work is a lesson in the art of acting."

He was born in Omaha, Nebraska. Following schooling at Shattuck Military Academy in Minnesota, he went to New York to try acting.

After a year at the Dramatic Workshop, he joined a summer stock company on Long Island, and was seen by an agent who helped him win a role in *I Remember Mama* on Broadway. There followed appearances in *Truckline Cafe, Candida* with Katharine Cornell and *A Flag Is Born* with Paul Muni. Then came *A Streetcar Named Desire* in which his portrayal of Stanley Kowalski electrified critics and led to his brilliant film career.

His screen performances include *The Men, A Streetcar Named Desire, Viva Zapata, Julius Caesar, The Teahouse of the August Moon, Guys and Dolls, Sayonara, On the Waterfront,* (for which he won an Academy Award). With *One Eyed Jacks* he made his debut as a director, and hopes to develop this talent further.

TREVOR HOWARD: Captain Bligh

The apex of a brilliant career is reached as the commander of the Bounty, after more than a decade of creating many memorable characterizations in an impressive list of British films. MUTINY ON THE BOUNTY marks his first appearance in a Hollywood produced motion picture.

He was born in Cliftonville, England. His father's business (he was an underwriter for Lloyd's of London) took the family all over the world.

At 18, he enrolled in the Royal Academy of Dramatic Arts where he was honored as "the finest actor" in his class. Upon graduation he went to London to make his leading man debut in *Revolt in a Reformatory*. This was followed by other roles (including two years of stardom in *French Without Tears*) and a few seasons of Shakespeare at Stratford-on-Avon. After World War II service, he began his film career by portraying a naval officer in *The Way Ahead*. Then came Noel Coward's *Brief Encounter*, and more than 20 other films, including such memorable ones as *So Well Remembered*, *The Third Man* and *Sons and Lovers* for which he won an Academy Award nomination.

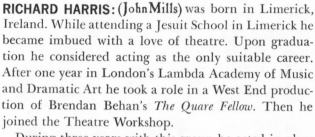

RICHARD HARRIS: (John Mills) was born in Limerick, Ireland. While attending a Jesuit School in Limerick he became imbued with a love of theatre. Upon graduation he considered acting as the only suitable career. After one year in London's Lambda Academy of Music and Dramatic Art he took a role in a West End production of Brendan Behan's *The Quare Fellow.* Then he joined the Theatre Workshop.

During three years with this group he acted in plays as varied as tragedies by Shakespeare and O'Casey to comedies by Kaufman and Hart.

For two years in London he portrayed the title role in *The Ginger Man.* He made his motion picture debut in *Shake Hands with the Devil,* has since become firmly established as a major star in such films as *The Long, the Short and the Tall* and *Guns of Navarone.*

HUGH GRIFFITH: (Alexander Smith) whose bearded Sheik in *Ben-Hur* won him an Academy Award, was born in North Wales.

While working as a bank clerk in London he won a scholarship to the Royal Academy of Dramatic Art.

His first professional role was in *Rhonda* in 1939, and except for six years in the British Armed Forces, he has been acting ever since. After the war he acted at Stratford-on-Avon, then starred on Broadway in *Legend of Lovers.* His performance as the father in *Look Homeward, Angel* won him wide acclaim on Broadway. Among his films have been *Exodus* and *The Counterfeit Traitor.*

RICHARD HAYDN: (William Brown) was born in London. He began his career as manager of a Gas Light and Coke Company's London office. When the office failed he devoted full time to acting. He made his stage debut with John Gielgud in a production of Chekov's *The Seagull.*

In 1938, he came to the United States to star with Beatrice Lillie in Noel Coward's *Set to Music* on Broadway. He made his film debut in *Charley's Aunt* and has created a variety of character portrayals in numerous films, among them *The Late George Apley, Forever Amber* and *Please Don't Eat the Daisies.* He has directed several films and written a best seller, *The Journal of Edwin Carp.*

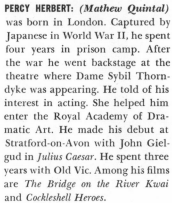

PERCY HERBERT: *(Mathew Quintal)* was born in London. Captured by Japanese in World War II, he spent four years in prison camp. After the war he went backstage at the theatre where Dame Sybil Thorndyke was appearing. He told of his interest in acting. She helped him enter the Royal Academy of Dramatic Art. He made his debut at Stratford-on-Avon with John Gielgud in *Julius Caesar.* He spent three years with Old Vic. Among his films are *The Bridge on the River Kwai* and *Cockleshell Heroes.*

GORDON JACKSON: *(Edward Birkett)* was born in Glasgow, Scotland, where his father was a school teacher. He began acting in radio plays. He studied engineering in college and continued acting on radio in Glasgow. He was signed because of his Scottish accent to make a film debut in *The Fireman Went to France.* He decided to continue acting, and after repertory work in Australia, starred in London's West End for four years in *Seagulls Over Sorrento.* Among his films are *Tight Little Island* and *Abandon Ship!*

NOEL PURCELL: *(William McCoy)* was born in Dublin, Ireland, where he became an apprentice to cabinet maker. He acted in church plays for the fun of it, and sometimes worked as an usher at the local music hall. In 1927 he was invited to play the lead in a musical review. Then he spent 10 years with a traveling company. He joined Dublin's Theatre Royal in 1939; starred in plays by Sean O'Casey, others. Among his films are *Odd Man Out, The Blue Lagoon* and *Lust for Life.*

DUNCAN LAMONT: *(John Williams)* was born in Balquidder, Scotland. His family moved to Portugal and then to South America. He returned to England for school, and while still a youngster performed with a traveling company which played Shakespeare. At 17 he entered the Royal Academy of Dramatic Arts. He served six years as a glider pilot in World War II. He has since starred in London plays and on television. Among his films are *The Golden Coach* and *Ben-Hur.*

CHIPS RAFFERTY: *(Michael Byrne)* was born in New South Wales, Australia. He worked as ranch hand and journalist. In 1938 while living on a cabin cruiser in Sydney, a friend offered him a role in the film *Ants in His Pants.* Except for four years in the Australian Air Force, he has been acting ever since. He has played in more than 40 pictures. Some were produced by his own company. Among his films are *Desert Rats* and *The Sundowners.*

ASHLEY COWAN: *(Samuel Mack)* born in London, entered show business as page boy at the famed Windmill Theatre and had his first chance at acting when he substituted for a performer who became ill. His first film was *Queen of Hearts.* He appeared with Danny Kaye on Broadway in *Let's Face It,* and has remained in the United States ever since. He spent five years in the U. S. Air Force. Among his films are *Snakepit* and *Sorry, Wrong Number.*

EDDIE BYRNE: *(John Fryer)* was born in Dublin. He left school to work and became a journalist. While appearing in amateur theatricals he was offered a role in *Peer Gynt* by Dublin's Gate Theatre. He decided to make acting his career and spent two years with the Abbey Theatre. He made his London debut in O'Casey's *Red Roses for Me* in 1946. He has since starred in a number of plays. Among his films are *Captain Boycott* and *Odd Man Out.*

TIM SEELY: *(Edward Young)* was born in London. His father was James Seely, successful gentleman farmer whose hobby was steeplechase riding and who rode three times in the Grand National. Young Tim, after attending Eton, entered the Royal Academy of Dramatic Art, interrupted his studies to serve in British Army for two years. He played the lead in the London production of *Tea and Sympathy.* Since has starred in more than 20 TV plays on BBC. Among his films are *The Poacher's Daughter* and *Please Turn Over.*

KEITH McCONNELL: *(James Morrison)* was born in Dublin. He left boarding school in England to join the Irish Army in 1943. After two years he returned to Dublin and joined the Gate Theatre to learn acting. He went to London in 1947 and while holding down his job, also made his film debut with Michael Rennie in *Idol of Paris.* In 1949, after playing in several British stage plays, he went to Hollywood. Among his films are *When Willie Comes Marching Home, Kim* and *Plymouth Adventure.*

And on the Island...

more than 10,000 Polynesian natives became actors for the first time in their lives. It was a case of doing what comes naturally, for in most of the scenes they were required to dance, laugh, fish and sail canoes.

Lovely Tarita, 19 year old daughter of a handsome fisherman on Bora Bora, won the part of the girl who captures the love of Fletcher Christian after a search that found talent agents visiting the principal islands in French Polynesia.

Born Taritatumi Teriipaia, she studied in a school operated by the French on Bora Bora until she was 17. Under contract to MGM she traveled to Hollywood on her first visit away from the islands. She still regards Bora Bora and Tahiti as her homes.

Matahiarii Tama, who makes his living fishing in the lagoons off Tahiti, was selected for the role of Chief Hitihiti. Once before, some 30 years ago, he deserted his fishing poles to play a leading role in "Tabu," the classic film about Polynesian life.

To portray Minarii, the noble Tahitian who accompanies Christian and the mutineers to Pitcairn, the producers chose Frank Silvera, brilliant West Indies actor. Since moving to Boston from Jamaica at the age of eight, Silvera has been acting.

He has starred in a number of plays in New York. In London in addition to acting in the West End, he lectured before Oxford University's Drama Society. He has played leading roles in a score of important films prior to MUTINY ON THE BOUNTY.

Tarita

Frank Silvera   Matahiarii

Aaron Rosenberg

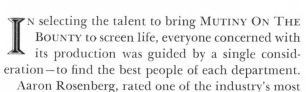

The Finest Talent

IN selecting the talent to bring MUTINY ON THE BOUNTY to screen life, everyone concerned with its production was guided by a single consideration—to find the best people of each department.

Aaron Rosenberg, rated one of the industry's most creative minds and one of its ablest producers, was considered the perfect choice as producer.

One of football's all time greats (he was an All American guard for three successive years at the University of Southern California), he entered motion pictures upon graduation from college, starting as an assistant director. As a producer he has gained fame as the creator of many memorable films, including among others: "Bend of the River," "The World in His Arms," "Winchester 73," "The Great Man" and the highly successful "The Glenn Miller Story."

Director Lewis Milestone brought to the project an inventive and resourceful talent that has been sharpened through years of directing a number of great motion pictures, including "The Front Page," "Rain," "Of Mice and Men" and "A Walk in the Sun." He won an Academy Award for "All Quiet on the Western Front," regarded by many as the finest anti-war film ever produced.

To write the screenplay, Charles Lederer was chosen for the herculean task of compressing the exciting and involved story of "the mutiny" into a script. Since 1931 Lederer has devoted most of his professional life to writing for the screen. Among his many scripts have been those for "The Front Page," "Topaze," "Comrade X," "I Was a Male War Bride," "Gentlemen Prefer Blondes" and "Tip on a Dead Jockey."

Bronislau Kaper, Polish born composer-pianist, whose imaginative music has enriched more than a dozen of the most successful films of recent years wrote the stirring musical score. Creator of such remembered melodies as the title tune from "San Francisco" and the Academy Award winning "Hi Lili, Hi Lo" from "Lili," he found the new assignment the

most challenging of his brilliant career. His score which incorporates themes based on Polynesian songs as well as sea chants, was recorded for the film by an enlarged MGM Symphony Orchestra with Robert Armbruster conducting.

Robert Surtees, whose brilliant camera work on "Ben-Hur" won him his third Academy Award, was named head cinematographer, with Harold Wellman engaged for additional photography. A photographic staff of fifteen experienced cameramen made the trip to Tahiti to assist in filming the picture in Ultra Panavision, a spectacular new 70 mm process.

Art direction was in the capable hands of George Davis and J. McMillan Johnson. The latter, whose specialty is creating sets for films with tropical background, spent more than a year and a half in Tahiti on the project. Henry Grace and Hugh Hunt, both MGM veterans, supervised the set decoration and

"Fletcher Christian" and camera

"Captain Bligh" between scenes

Director Lewis Milestone

Richard Harris catches a shark from deck of the BOUNTY

special visual effects were contributed by A. Arnold Gillespie, Lee LeBlanc and Robert R. Hoag.

James C. Havens, for many years the foremost director of action scenes depicting life on the sea, was in charge of second unit direction. In addition, he supervised construction of the Bounty in Nova Scotia and sailed with her to Tahiti, where he and an intrepid camera crew spent many weeks filming the difficult sea sequences.

John McSweeney, one of Hollywood's most expert film editors, compressed the thousands and thousands of exposed celluloid frames into the final picture.

The costumes, both native and naval, were designed by Moss Mabry, a two time Academy Award nominee with Charles K. Hagedon serving as color consultant. Hair styles were created by Mary Keats and Makeup by William Tuttle.

Franklin Milton was recording supervisor, in charge of the large crew of sound experts who spent many months in the South Seas recording the chants of the natives and the exciting sounds on the islands.

To stage the elaborate dance number which is the highlight of the feast sequence, choreographer Hamil Petroff was selected. He searched Tahiti and neighboring islands to discover the finest dancers. The 76 girls and 36 boys he finally chose worked for weeks to perfect the intricate dance they perform for Captain Bligh and his men.

These, along with more than 100 of the finest film artisans from Hollywood, London and Paris, were the men and women who brought their vast technical knowledge and skill into play to create the colorful backgrounds (with an assist from nature, of course) against which the actors could perform.

William Bligh, from an old print

The Log of The Bounty

Being excerpts from William Bligh's Log of the Proceedings of His Majesty's Armed Vessel Bounty in a Voyage to the South Seas.

(as taken from the official manuscript given by Bligh to the British Admiralty and still preserved in London.)

AUGUST 16, 1787 . . .
I had the honor to receive my Appointment from the Lord Commissioners of the Admiralty to Command His Majesty's Armed Vessel Bounty, forthwith to put her in Commission and to use the utmost dispatch to complete her for a voyage to remote parts.

OCTOBER 9th . . .
Ready, Stored and Victualled for 18 months and with a Pilot on board proceeded from Deptford to Longreach where was brought to me all the Gunners Stores, four Carriages, four Pounders and 10 Swivels, with the necessary number of Small Arms.

OCTOBER 15th . . .
I received my Orders to proceed to Spithead but will not sail for days yet.

OCTOBER 24th . . .
Until this date could not get into the Downs, where meeting with Contrary Winds I was still not able to comply with my Orders.

NOVEMBER 4th . . .
After much bad weather I anchored at Spithead and Moored.

NOVEMBER 24th . . .
Lord Hood gave me my final Orders to Proceed to Sea. I now made application for my People to be paid their two Months Advance.

NOVEMBER 28th . . .
After the People received their Advance, unmoored and worked out to St. Helens with the Wind at the South, where we were Obliged to Anchor.

⚓ ⚓ ⚓

(Editor's Note: Owing to severe and contrary winds, the ship could not get down the English Channel and there was a delay which Bligh described in detail in an angry letter he wrote on December 10th to Duncan Campbell, West Indies trader and former owner of the Bounty. Among other things, he declared:

"If there is any punishment that ought to be inflicted on a set of men for neglect, I am sure it ought on the Admiralty for my three weeks' detention at this place during a fine fair wind which carried all outward bound ships clear of the Channel but me, who wanted it most. This has made my task a very arduous one indeed if I am to round Cape Horn. I know not how to promise myself any success and yet I must do it if the ship will stand it at all or I suppose my character will be at stake. Had Lord Howe sweetened this difficult task by giving me promotion I should have been satisfied, but he has done it with a Lieutenant Moorsom of the Ariel, bound on a Voyage to the East Indies, whose difficulties are not likely to be any way equal to those I am to encounter.)

⚓ ⚓ ⚓

DECEMBER 16th . . .
Strong Gales and Squally with heavy Rain at times. Cleaned Ship below and Served fresh Meat to the People. Mustered all People and saw that they were

Clean. Received on board 10 Casks of Beer. Read the Articles of War to Ships Company.

DECEMBER 24th . . .
Squally with Sleet. One of the People in furling the Main Tp Gt. sail fell Over and was saved by Catching hold of the Main T. Mast Stay by which he came down, not hurt at all. A Sea struck us on the larboard Quarter and some of the bread has got damaged. Ordered all Wet Cloaths to be taken by the Fire.

DECEMBER 25th . . .
The Gales begin to abate a little but still very Squally with Hail. This being Christmas Day I ordered an Allowance of Rum to be served to each person and Beef and Plum Pudding for Dinner.

DECEMBER 26th . . .
Moderate and fair Wr. which allowed us to spend our Christmas pleasantly. A Fine Moon.

DECEMBER 27th . . .
A Storm of Wind with most Violent Squalls. Also snow and sleet.
A very heavy Sea which broke the foremast Chock of the Boats to pieces and Stove all the Boats, it was with utmost difficulty and Risk that they were saved from being Washed Overboard, the Waist Boards on both Sides were Washed Away and we were an entire Sea on Deck.
The great hardship with small Ships in such Weather as this is that we cannot light a fire to dress Victuals, which has been our Case today. I therefore Ordered Grog to the People in addition to their Beer to make up for their Wet uncomfortable Situation. Seven of our half Hogsheads of Beer, all of which were full, were Washed Overboard.

JANUARY 11th . . .
Moderate Breezes and Clear Wr.
Ordered my people to be at three watched and gave the charge of the Third Watch to Mr. Fletcher Christian, one of the Mates.
Some time for relaxation and Mirth is absolutely necessary, and I have considered it so much so that after 4 o'clock the Evening is laid aside for their Amusement and dancing. I had great difficulty before I left England to get a Man to play the Violin and I preferred at last to take One two thirds Blind than come without one.
As 2/3 allowance of bread is as much as Men generally consume I ordered them to be put on it this day, and as their Water is all filtered through Drip-

Trevor Howard as Captain Bligh

stones, which I have procured for that purpose, few Seamen and Officers I may venture to Say, can ever boast of more Comforts at Sea.

(NOTE: *Bligh's confidence that his men would boast of their "Comforts at Sea" proved him not the best of prophets but his meticulous log, continued throughout his voyage on the Bounty and even in the openboat, remains a document of uncommon interest revealing the personality and thoughts of a most remarkable man.*)

⚓ ⚓ ⚓

DIAGRAM BY R. W. NICHOLSON, NATIONAL GEOGRAPHIC STAFF © N.G.S.

Bounty's sail plan

1—Jib. 2—Fore-topmast staysail. 3—Foresail. 4—Fore-topsail. 5—Fore-topgallant. 6—Fore-royal. 7—Mainsail. 8—Main-topsail. 9—Main-topgallant. 10—Main-royal. 11—Mizzen topsail. 12—Mizzen-topgallant. 13—Mizzen-royal. 14—Spanker. 15—Foremast. 16—Mainmast. 17—Mizzenmast. 18—Launch. 19—Bowsprit.

"There'll be no more killing aboard this ship . . ."

And from the log of the new H.M.S. Bounty as kept by Captain Ellsworth Coggins on voyage from Lunenburg, Nova Scotia to Tahiti:

OCTOBER 24 . . .
Sailed from Lunenburg under cloudy skies after farewell ceremonies at pier attended by several thousand well wishers. Seas heavy.

OCTOBER 27 . . .
Saluted Queen Mary at dawn. Despite early hour many passengers lined deck to wave greetings. Seas still heavy. Crew all well.

NOVEMBER 8 . . .
Luis Marden, Foreign Editor of National Geographic Magazine, hammered into the hull a bronze sheathing nail from original Bounty which he had brought up from bottom on diving expedition off Pitcairn.

NOVEMBER 12 . . .
Wind picked up and blew from nearly ahead, so could not use the square sails efficiently. Set fore and aft sails: main topmast staysail and spanker.

"His most gracious Majesty, King George, has ordered me present his compliments to King Hitihiti..."

"What are those deserters doing out of irons?"

NOVEMBER 20...
Crossed Equator at longitude 102 degrees 50.0'. Neptune came aboard over port bow, sat on throne on midships hatch while 15 neophytes were lathered with mixture concocted by cook and surgeon.

NOVEMBER 21...
Course SW 1/2, wind SSE, force 3. Slight sea.

DECEMBER 4...
Arrived under bright skies at Matavaii Bay in Tahiti and used same anchorage as Bligh. Received warm greeting from natives and members of film unit.

Marlon Brando and Tahitian friend

Mrs. James Norman Hall, widow of one of the authors of the book upon which the film is based, was a frequent visitor to the set in Tahiti, where she has lived most of her life.

Her son, Conrad Hall, was an assistant cameraman on the production and her son-in-law, Nick Rutgers, served as a consultant on the unit.

⚓

For one Tahitian maiden love won out over Hollywood during the making of the film. Cast in an important role, she was wooed and won by a French soldier stationed on the island. When he was transferred to Algeria she went along to become his wife even though the picture was still before the cameras. Her role had to be recast and the scenes she had done reshot.

⚓

Another Tahitian girl in the cast fell in love with Wayne Dewar, young Nova Scotian who was a member of the Bounty's crew. When the ship sailed back to America, she flew to Canada and in Halifax settled down to become his wife and begin a life about as far removed from that to which a Tahitian girl is accustomed as one could imagine.

⚓

PRODUCTION NOTES

Assistant Director Reggie Callow had a unique linguistic problem when issuing the daily call for native girls to appear in scenes in Tahiti. A sampling of first names of more than 50 girls who have small roles reveals: Marabayshi, Tefaaoro, Faatiarau, Ahuroa, Teriitemihau and Manitearo. On the other hand there was an Agnes, a Marie and an Emily to help balance the ledger.

⚓

Captain Donald MacIntyre, who served as technical adviser for sea sequences in the production, is credited with sinking seven German U-boats while commanding a British destroyer in World War II.

⚓

Almost the entire population of Bora Bora (approximately 1,000) participated in the stone fishing sequence. Three quarters of the residents in the island's only town of Vaitapo gave their homes to the members of the company who spent time in their midst.

⚓

Tarita and her fisherman father

Relaxing between scenes

"Admit it—you never saw a lovelier creature . . ."

"A delightful evening, excellency . . ."

The bread fruit which indirectly led to the famous mutiny, grows on trees and is shaped something like a cocoanut. The trees, sometimes rising to 60 feet, need a hot, humid climate and rich soil in which to take root. The plant contains a firm yellow pulp which is moist and quite sweet. It is still a favorite with Tahitians. But, ironically, when Bligh eventually returned to Tahiti and successfully transplanted the plants to Jamaica, the plantation slaves for whom it was intended as a cheap food, turned up their noses and refused to eat it.

⚓

The original Bounty actually began her career as the Bethia. That was her name when the British Admiralty bought her from Duncan Campbell, West Indies trader, in 1787 for the sum of 1,950 pounds. Refitted at Deptford at a cost of 4,456 pounds, she was rechristened and armed with four short four-pounders and ten swivel guns, mostly for protection against hostile natives who might be encountered in the South seas.

⚓

Olof Olsson, one of the few remaining experts in the lost art of sail and rope rigging and a 25 year veteran of MGM's props department, was in charge of all the intricate rigging aboard the Bounty, consisting of miles of hawsers, ropes and lesser lines necessary to put the Bounty under sail. In total, Olsson handle what amounted to a 15-ton ball of rope, varying in size from 2½ inches to 1/16th inches in diameter. ⚓

Bronislau Kaper, whose imaginative musical scores have enriched more than a dozen successful motion pictures of recent years, was chosen to compose the musical score for the film, and for the project, Kaper went to Tahiti, gathered native musicians and musical instruments and recorded countless Tahitian songs and chants to give himself the proper mood for writing a score which would be suitable.

⚓

The 10,000 square yards of canvas that went into the 18 different sails aboard H.M.S. Bounty were sewn by 70-year-old Charlie Hebb, who has lived all his life in Lunenburg, Nova Scotia, and is one of the few men left in the world today whose craft is sail making. Seated in his little shop, which he opened 50 years ago, he devoted six months to fashioning the royals, the top gallants and the various other sails that carry the three-masted ship through the seas.

⚓

Two natives of Tahiti, Leo Langamazino and Aurora Natua, worked closely with the company to insure authenticity of all Polynesian sequences. They are considered two of the finest experts in the world on subject of the Tahitian people and their customs.

⚓

"The sextant . . . I left it in my cabin . . ."

Fate of the Bounty and Her Crew

⚓ ⚓ ⚓

FLETCHER CHRISTIAN

He died on Pitcairn Island shortly after the mutiny. For many years rumors persisted in England that he had somehow escaped the island and returned to his mother country. His descendants still live on Pitcairn Island today.

⚓ ⚓ ⚓

CAPTAIN BLIGH

After miraculously surviving the trip in a small boat across open seas to Timor following mutiny on H.M.S. Bounty, Bligh continued his career with the Royal Navy, serving with distinction. From 1805 until 1808, he served as Governor of New South Wales in Australia, and later became a Vice Admiral.

" 'Morning, Ned. Sleep well?"

"This is what we have come for, your Excellency—the breadfruit."

"... Isn't it amazing ... such a delicate sprig—with the power to feed a continent!"

MEN WHO REMAINED ON THE BOUNTY

Two died in Tahiti; nine died on Pitcairn Island, the barren rock where they had sailed on the Bounty to escape the wrath of the English Crown; four were drowned in a shipwreck; seven died free men in England where they were taken after being discovered on Tahiti by the British. Three men who were brought from Tahiti to England stood trial for their part in the mutiny, and were hanged.

BLIGH'S LOYAL SEAMEN

One was stoned to death by natives during a stop at an uncharted island on the open boat voyage to Timor; five died shortly after the small boat miraculously reached Timor in the Dutch East Indies following the 3,618-mile voyage; one died in a shipwreck while returning home to England; eleven others reached their homes in the British Isles safely.

H.M.S. BOUNTY

The vessel was burned and sunk off Pitcairn Island by the mutineers who did not want the Bounty used as an escape ship for anyone in the mutiny party.

Fletcher Thursday October Christian on Pitcairn today

Trevor Howard with Mrs. James Norman Hall, widow of BOUNTY co-author

Descendants of mutineers living in Tahiti today, all of whom appear in the film